THE BUSINESS

THE COLORADO PRIZE FOR POETRY

Strike Anywhere, by Dean Young
selected by Charles Simic, 1995

Summer Mystagogia, by Bruce Beasley
selected by Charles Wright, 1996

The Thicket Daybreak, by Catherine Webster
selected by Jane Miller, 1997

Palma Cathedral, by Michael White
selected by Mark Strand, 1998

Popular Music, by Stephen Burt
selected by Jorie Graham, 1999

Design, by Sally Keith
selected by Allen Grossman, 2000

A Summer Evening, by Geoffrey Nutter
selected by Jorie Graham, 2001

Chemical Wedding, by Robyn Ewing
selected by Fanny Howe, 2002

Goldbeater's Skin, by G. C. Waldrep
selected by Donald Revell, 2003

Whethering, by Rusty Morrison
selected by Forrest Gander, 2004

Frayed escort, by Karen Garthe
selected by Cal Bedient, 2005

Carrier Wave, by Jaswinder Bolina
selected by Lyn Hejinian, 2006

Brenda Is in the Room and Other Poems,
by Craig Morgan Teicher
selected by Paul Hoover, 2007

One Sun Storm, by Endi Bogue Hartigan
selected by Martha Ronk, 2008

The Lesser Fields, by Rob Schlegel
selected by James Longenbach, 2009

Annulments, by Zach Savich
selected by Donald Revell, 2010

Scared Text, by Eric Baus
selected by Cole Swensen, 2011

Family System, by Jack Christian
selected by Elizabeth Willis, 2012

Intimacy, by Catherine Imbriglio
selected by Stephen Burt, 2013

Supplice, by T. Zachary Cotler
selected by Claudia Keelan, 2014

The Business, by Stephanie Lenox
selected by Laura Kasischke, 2015

THE BUSINESS

poems

Stephanie Lenox

THE CENTER FOR LITERARY PUBLISHING
COLORADO STATE UNIVERSITY

For information about permission to reproduce
selections from this book, write to
The Center for Literary Publishing
attn: Permissions
9105 Campus Delivery
Colorado State University
Fort Collins, Colorado 80523-9105.

Printed in the United States of America.

Library of Congress Cataloging-in-Publication Data
Lenox, Stephanie.
[Poems. Selections]
The business : poems / Stephanie Lenox.
pages ; cm. -- (The Colorado prize for poetry)
ISBN 978-1-885635-47-1 (pbk. : alk. paper) -- ISBN 978-1-885635-48-8 (electronic)
I. Title.
PS3612.E5557A6 2015
811'.6--dc23

2015029487

The paper used in this book meets the minimum requirements of the
American National Standard for Information Sciences-Permanence of Paper
for Printed Library Materials, ANSI Z39.48-1984.

1 2 3 4 5 19 18 17 16 15

For Charlie

CONTENTS

STASIMON

EXODE

PROLOGUE

Meanwhile telephones crouch, getting ready to ring
In locked-up offices, and all the uncaring
Intricate rented world begins to rouse.

—Philip Larkin, "Aubade"

AUBADE FOR THE FIRST WEEK

It's all their fault, those naked two,
blinking into dawn's sadistic glow.

Let there be light, God said,
and there was light. Too much of it.

Your fig leaf's crooked, spake Eve.
Adam fashioned a necktie from a vine.

Biblical trendsetters, they were caught
pants down before the invention of pants!

Ruined for good, they lugged those dust-
filled briefcases to work.

Because of them we stumble
toward the closet, bruising head and heel,

marrying shirt to pants, socks to shoes.
We busy ourselves with preparation.

For better or worse, we toil over toiletries,
rake eyes open with the mascara wand.

A crooked seam, button missed, tag
turned out—so many opportunities

for failure. On the sink's edge
the blob of toothpaste hardens.

Where are the keys? Where are
the goddamn keys to the kingdom?

We count the nicks and nylon runs.
We would give anything to go back

to bed. All day long we await
the zipper's tiny momentary shush—

all that must be done and
undone in each other's hands.

THE BUSINESS

The tractor in the field
does not take things personally.

It is not affronted by the way
wheat bends before it, all that luscious weakness.

There is no mind, just a motor,
a servitude of parts churning

politely together. The oily smoke
is only smoke, nothing more.

If steered by the farmer's hand
off track into rutted earth,

it will not cry out,
O thou hast sorely done me wrong!

No, it takes a person
to take things personally.

Whatever the farmer has planted, it will cut.
It will devastate the field into harvest.

When time comes and the farmer
abandons it in a far corner of the field,

it feels nothing. How can anyone
take things personally out here

beneath the blue, unambiguous sky?
The tractor cannot choose to stop or go.

It cannot hate the hand that guides it.
Do not feel sorry for the blade

or for the mice that flee from it
or for the slow, dumb grouse—

it should have known better.
There can be no tragedy here

unless you see it—*you,*
sweet pathetic ladder of bones

leaning against that blighted tree.

ON MYTHOLOGY

Every story begins with a slight—
golden-apple hand grenade tossed into the crowd.

Until that moment, no one is thinking about ideals.
Being perfect is simply a way to pass the time.

Then enters Doubt, a chorus of questions,
someone new on the scene, an intern, perhaps.

Add fire or flood, a touch of unfaithfulness.
Damage that must be paid for again and again.

Pain at the center of all story. Pain. At the center.
Oh, how we love our stories.

A journey, a war, a mesmerizing face.
The myth is that we think it will be different.

Character and plot: one rock, one endless, bone-heaped hill.
To be angry is to take your place among the gods.

REJOICE IN THE PETTY THIEVERY OF OFFICE SUPPLIES

after Christopher Smart

For you are not the first to take what is not yours.
For the ballpoint's grip aligns perfectly with your hand.
For the string of paper clips makes an elegant accessory.
For work begets more work, and in the meantime, you need a box of staples.
For there are staplers and then there are HEAVY-DUTY staplers.
For you can never have enough sticky notes.
For the card stock is beautiful and thick and deserves a higher purpose.
For you have an insatiable desire for paper products.
For the office receives an incredible deal for ordering in bulk.
For you are the one who does all the ordering.
For your children are returning to school and this is a form of tuition assistance.
For there will be no raises this year.
For the manager kept you after hours three days in a row to review the budget that should have been completed last month, and your compensation is manila folders.
For the letter opener sings with meaning.
For all the Pilot® Precise Rolling Ball V5 Retractable pens at home have gone dry.
For your son is doing a science project and requires transparencies.
For it is just a pen, not a pension.
For to take what you need is an implicit reward of work.
For everyone makes mistakes and has need for Wite-Out®.
For one in every dozen envelopes belongs to you.
For one in every dozen binder clips of every size belongs to you.
For one ream in every box of paper is owed to you.
For you have given your eyes over to the computer monitor.
For your wrists ache at night with tendonitis.
For your hands have been lacerated by the filing stack.
For your manuscript has been printed and copied at the boss's expense.
For the boss is a generous patron of the arts, though unwittingly.
For the boss has a leather portfolio with engraved initials, and this desk calendar you've received in lieu of a Christmas bonus, what a piece of crap.
For your boss does not even know how to turn on the fax machine.
For having considered the boss and yourself, you will consider your coworker.

For you have given your ears daily to the inane lyrics of your office mate's beloved country station.
For you have endured the smell of trout being reheated in the break room.
For you are the only one to refill the pot of coffee once it has been emptied.
For there is an overabundance of highlighters, and you are just trying to ease the burden.
For your favorite crosscut shredder is too large to carry home.
For no one knows what happened to all the mechanical pencils.
For you have written the manual that no one will read.
For ink is costly and dear.
For the file folders index your bills, which is your work after work.
For you have given your life to this company, and in return you should never have to buy another two-pocket portfolio.
For there is a price to pay.
For it is called attrition.
For it is called diminishing returns.
For it is called a substitute for employee morale.
For you spend more time in your rolling chair than in your own bed.
For this is expected and part of the annual budget.
For the envelopes with small clasps hold their contents firmly.
For the envelopes with windows are not cheap.
For to recycle is to show your respect for the planet.
For you cannot live without a three-hole punch.
For the legal pads have proved their worth.
For firstly, work will come home with you either way, in spirit or in satchel.
For secondly, you fear that erasable pens will become relics of the past.
For thirdly, you are relieving the office of overstock.
For fourthly, you have sharpened your pencils to the finest point.
For fifthly, you have always wanted a date stamp.
For sixthly, you are liberating the rubber bands and pushpins from their uselessness.
For seventhly, you could be downsized at any time, and it is good to have reserves.
For eighthly, you are assembling a portfolio of your outstanding performances.
For ninthly, you will be blamed for taking them whether you have or not.

For tenthly, it is your job to supply for your family.
For you have considered leaving the company if it weren't for their 20-lb. cotton fiber premium white paper with watermark.
For a man or woman can be measured by their assortment of writing utensils.
For the supply closet only has so much space.
For the solar-powered calculator cannot function properly indoors.
For the message pads come in useful when communicating with your spouse.
For you would laminate the world.
For you love all office supplies equally.
For no one but you really knows what they're worth.

MANAGEMENT SENDS OUT A MEMO THANKING ITS CHAIRS

Without you, buttress
of heavy bottoms,
where would we be?
You twirl beneath
our fingertips, adjust
to all manner of heights.

Chariot of efficiency
bracing us for the day's work,
if not for you
we'd pace from room
to room, unable to prop
our sagging bodies upright,
unable to hold
important meetings.

There's no real skill
in bearing up—
it's just the way
you've been engineered,
to amend and minister
to our needs,
to stay put.

On this day we praise you
(since praise is rare
for doing what you're told,
but thank heavens you do)
because where else
would we sit?

O conscript, underling,
coordinating throne—
how little we think of you.

Cast us toward the work station,
lean back into this corporate tango,
rolling toward the copier,
the ringing phone.
You make it look easy.

This office could not run
without you. On wheels—*whee!*—
you spin like a globe,
you sigh when we press your levers.

SECRETARIES IN HEAVEN

This is their new office:
                                        alphabetizing clouds,

creating a database of prayers received,
prayers answered, shooing
cherubs off the Xerox,
                                        the green beam
churning out one perfect copy after another.

They have taught the saints how to multitask;
their pearl-drop fingernails
take dictation.

                        There is no need for correction fluid
since they've arrived.
                                        Heaven couldn't be better.

The souls over their endless coffee mugs
joke about who's really in charge.

Death has been delegated to them completely—
they're just so *efficient*—the pink stubs
of their Number Twos
                                        descending from the heavens
in a swift swipe of erasure.

The afterlife requires such meticulousness.

It is their business,
perpetually sending out memos to the living.
They know everything under the sun.

Calves bejeweled
in shimmering nylon that never runs,
eyelids iridescent,

they whisper in their cubicles—
they know who's next.

Here in this chorus
of machines, the tone-deaf copier,

the cacophony of the fax, the Golden Swingline's
thump and thud,
they wait for us,
their round rumps on roller chairs that skim
across the great
desperate spaces—so organized!
so detail oriented!—singing, *Hallelujah*,

this is Heaven, please hold—

THE TASK

The bowl is empty
and it must be filled.

I will set a reminder
to remind you.

I will remind myself
to tell you this:

remember, you must
fill it if it is empty.

This is your job.

I will help you
to remember the bowl,
how it must be filled,

not just today,
but in perpetuity.

And if it is empty,
I will remind you

that the bowl, empty,
needs to be filled.

Filling the bowl
must be your first task,

and I will help you
remember. The bowl

tends toward emptiness.
You have responsibilities.

You must prove yourself.
Will you fill it?

SAUSAGE IS THE NATURAL OUTCOME OF EFFICIENT BUTCHERY

We don't want to think too hard
about where these things come from.
Organ meat, animal fat, blood . . .
in each a trace of the questionable,
an economy of slaughter.

This butchery we were raised on,
beast boiled down to remnants,
slurry of leftovers. We must not think
of the blade, every turn
an opportunity for disease or worse.

Victorious in battle, Greeks dined on it.
In 500 BC, Epicharmus wrote about it—
impossible now to say comedy or tragedy.
But if I had to guess, I'd say comedy.
For the humans, at least.

In after-school cartoons the mouse binds
and gags the unlucky cat with a chain
of sausages he will never eat. *That* is tragedy.
The schoolteacher says, *You are what you eat*.
And so we are. One raw bag linked to another.

Onions weep onto a white plate.
I said do not think of the blade.
How beautiful the rancid patina,
that opalescence, these few delicious
indignities we manage to survive.

FAX MACHINES ARE PASSING FROM OUR LIVES

any moment I'll fall
on my side and drum my toes
like a typewriter . . .
—Philip Levine, "Animals Are Passing from Our Lives"

I will have to explain these things someday
to my children, like the misguided tattoo
or the fact that, while I did inhale, it only
amplified my natural state of paranoia.

I can't remember the last time I used one.
Now that it's gone I regret not taking the time
to learn its complex array of buttons
and what they were meant to do.

The cacophony of its gears is a long-gone
song taking me back to the good old days
filled with breath mints, a steady paycheck,
and the potted plant crowding the cubicle.

I remember that colleague, the one
I so detested, those passionate nights spent
filing dream insults and grinding my teeth
to chalk. Wasn't it romantic?

How long has it been since I've felt that way
about anyone?

His exaggerated guffaw followed me
everywhere. His pasty sneer seared itself
to the back of my eyelids. I thought
I would never be free of him.

It's hard to imagine, but even that awkward
behemoth accumulates nostalgia
much as it once collected dust, squatting
in the corner of the office, belching junk.

ON METAPHOR

Your boss is an ass. Your pay, shit.
Each day feels like two, every task pointing
to another: the nine-to-five multiplying paperwork.
No wonder you're tired, two bosses on your back,
the boss of *what is* and the boss of *what could be.*

Of course, you don't get paid more
for taking on new work. It's the price, you say,
of competence. Your job is a ship
propelling you forward. It is a lead weight, a bird.
No one knows what's in your briefcase,
not even you, but you carry it back and forth,
part of the uniform, a symbol of duty.

A raise is not just more money. The coffee pot
is a sacred monument. One floor above,
one floor below, someone like you worries
over his retirement, rearranges pens,
reads a headline of national progress
then turns to the photo of a car wreck.

On your own, you have no authority:
each decision you make must be approved
by another, and for that you're glad,
sharing the weight if something goes wrong
but also the glory if all goes right, the business
of making something else for someone else,
endlessly generous, the work of work.

EMPLOYEE MANUAL FOR MORTALS

If you are too beautiful
and poets belabor the symmetry
of your face,
you will be punished.
Beauty must be kept
in a locked room, desire
in another.

If you have taken a lover,
and that lover is your sister
or your father or a ray
of golden light, don't be surprised
if something really bad
happens to you.

Let's just say you find a newborn
on a hillside. Don't pick it up.
No matter how cute it is.
Just don't do it. Ever.

Love is dangerous.
It will change into a tree,
or you will drown in it.

Shy away from trinkets or swans
or tantalizing songs. It might be a good idea
to poke your eyes out now
before things get any worse.

Listen, you are not the hero here.
If you read more, you might understand
that the letter you are carrying
contains your death sentence.

You should not have to be told
such things: to fail like this, quietly,
with limbs and bowels intact,
might be your fate.

Don't brag about your archery skills.
Know the target by watching
where the arrows fall.
If you are rescuing your lover from Hades,
and you are told not to look back—
brother, sister, don't look back.

PARODE

Do not drink the ink.

—Instructions on a printer cartridge

TEAMWORK

Let's make this the best day ever.
Let's get to work.
Let's look at how we can improve the process.
Let's create a flowchart, a spreadsheet, a PowerPoint presentation.
Let's make it sparkle.
Let's really make it shine.
Let's all remember to fill out our vacation requests.
Let's call tech support and see what they have to say.
Let's put in 110%.
Let's make it a team effort.
Let's make it look like we do work around here.
Let's give it up for Carl in the corner office.
Let's give it a rest.
Let's recall that there is no "I" in teamwork.
Let's proofread the memo before it goes out next time.
Let's take a break now.
Let's break for lunch.
Let's meet for coffee to discuss the new hiring process.
Let's form a committee.
Let's have some fun.
Let's not have the support staff take more than two fifteen-minute breaks per shift.
Let's not see that happen again.
Let's all sing "Happy Birthday" now.
Let's sign the card for the accountant whose wife was just diagnosed with breast cancer.
Let's cheer up Dan with a plant. A philodendron, maybe. Nothing too girly.
Let's figure out who's responsible for the mess we're in.
Let's purchase a new copy machine.
Let's have a meeting about it.
Let's not be here when he gets back.
Let's have a serious talk about what it means to work here.
Let's not be like that.
Let's be more fastidious about emptying the trash. We shouldn't have fruit flies.

Let's write a report about what needs to be done next.
Let's discuss the report in our next budget meeting.
Let's get this done right away.
Let's be happy that the situation isn't worse.
Let's announce the new position at the next staff meeting.
Let's call it ignorance.
Let's keep it under wraps.
Let's keep it on the down low.
Let's be careful to have none of this in writing.
Let's not say a word until we speak to our lawyers.
Let's make fun of lawyers in our next meeting.
Let's agree not to discuss this until we know exactly what we're dealing with.
Let's stay home and pretend we're sick.
Let's not wish we had something different.
Let's all remember to say thank you to our support staff.
Let's put this in the minutes. Sharon, did you get that?
Let's roll with the punches.
Let's shoot some pool after work.
Let's take this outside.
Let's be reasonable here.
Let's behave like adults.
Let's not kid ourselves. There will be no raises this year.
Let's take it easy on the microwave popcorn, everyone.
Let's act first, beg forgiveness later.
Let's call the groundskeeper to remove the pigeon from the corridor before the shit literally hits the fan. Har-har!
Let's say something nice about the folks in HR for a change.
Let's consider the lilies. They toil not. Neither do they spin.
Let's leave our politics at the door, boys.
Let's not clutter our desks with too many picture frames.
Let's try to limit the number of personal phone calls.
Let's not allow resentment to run our lives.

Let's remember this is an office, not your home.
Let's treat each other with respect. We're family here.
Let's pick up where we left off at the last meeting.
Let's add this to the agenda.
Let's hope for the best. Suzie is a strong gal.
Let's clean the fridge and take home all Tupperware.
Let's not permit mold to grow in the Mr. Coffee.
Let's take all the shredding to the bins at noon.
Let's run some figures on the latest report.
Let's get some notice from the bigwigs.
Let's give it a shot. See if it works.
Let's hold our tongues around you-know-who.
Let's not wish him ill.
Let's not bad-mouth the weasel down the hall. Even if he deserves it.
Let's set a date for the next meeting to discuss the meeting before last.
Let's only use all caps if we REALLY WANT TO MAKE A POINT.
Let's limit the number of sticky notes we buy next month. Someone has been abusing the supply closet.
Let's return the spoons to the staff lounge so that others can use them, thank you very much.
Let's find a more productive way to bring up interpersonal issues.
Let's remember there is no such thing as a stupid question.
Let's think before we speak next time.
Let's discuss it in the next meeting.
Let's make sure we're all clear on this. Are we?
Let's go back to the beginning.
Let's hear what accounting has to say first.
Let's let the CFO make the final call.
Let's change the channel. We've seen this one before.
Let's not talk about your gallbladder.
Let's not talk about your daughter's braces.
Let's not talk about your softball team.
Let's not talk about the car accident that killed four teenagers, threw their bodies to the

wind. Such a waste.
Let's not talk about your six-toed cat. No, not again.
Let's not talk about your well-trained dog.
Let's put on some socks now. Where did the piggies go?
Let's put on some pants.
Let's pick out a shirt. You like the blue one? OK, let's wear the blue one.
Let's comb our hair. Aren't we so pretty?
Let's say bye-bye. *Bye-bye!*
Let's Google the new guy.
Let's just say Barb had a few too many.
Let's move the meeting to next Wednesday.
Let's not mourn forever. Diane led a good life.
Let's read aloud from the testament of John.
Let's get a drink before going back to work.
Let's consult the dictionary.
Let's just say her haircut is not the most flattering style for her shape of face. Someone ought to say something.
Let's not weep.
Let's find out for whom the bell tolls.
Let's have one hundred years of solitude.
Let's get someone to do something about the leaves of grass.
Let's start a book club, shall we?
Let's move the meeting to next week, just this once.
Let's make it official.
Let's say we didn't know anything about the project and when Janine starts to freak let's all yell, *Psych!*
Let's not and say we did.
Let's just say she hasn't been the same since the phone call. You know, *the call.*
Let's dance, dance, dance.
Let's boogie down.
Let's pretend this never happened.
Let's blame it on the allergy season.

Let's blame it on the cleaning lady.
Let's blame it on divorce or the threat of divorce.
Let's blame it on the temp with bad breath.
Let's take off our clothes.
Let's just stay home tonight.
Let's go to the ocean. A roadtrip. Get out of town.
Let's turn down the heat in here.
Let's have another doctor check it out.
Let's not rush into things.
Let's move the meeting to Friday.
Let's all plan on being here.
Let's get the paperwork done and in the mail by five o'clock today.
Let's think about this for a moment.
Let's assume he knows what he's talking about: what's our next step?
Let's take care to have the office properly secured. We should be able to remember to lock the files.
Let's all hear a round of applause for Suzie, employee of the month.
Let's not pretend this is about war and peace.
Let's have a mediator come in to work this out.
Let's remember there are many different ways to *communicate*.
Let's remember the Mars/Venus thing.
Let's remember not to stereotype.
Let's all be open-minded this quarter.
Let's not dig our own grave.
Let's not be martyrs here.
Let's not pretend we are saints.
Let's take a walk. I have something to tell you in private.
Let's not get upset about this. It was a matter of time.
Let's leave quietly. Suzie will help you collect your things.
Let's be on our way.
Let us describe in detail how they each deserted us one by one until only Suzie was left in her cube with her certificate and her ergonomic chair.

Let us remember to be grateful.
Let us see what love can do.
Let us not deny the pleasures of the flesh.
Let us abhor what is wicked.
Let us deport suspects to nations who might torture them.
Let us face the facts.
Let us go softly.
Let us show you the wonders of Viagra.
Let us tell you about the best software available for your computer.
Let us hear from you.
Let us pray that the darkest hour has passed.
Let us always Thank God It's Friday.
Let us forget the past.
Let us forget that little nonsense with the gun.
Let us all forget the Christmas party.
Let's all unite and celebrate together on this most blessed of occasions.
Let's have it.
Let's make a deal.
Let's talk about depression.
Let's talk about the best dental plan.
Let's talk about deadlines.
Let's talk to the boss about a promotion.
Let's talk about the boss—what a *b-i-t-c-h*.
Let's talk about insects and how to eradicate them.
Let's talk business.
Let's call it a night.

EPISODES

Ice cubes do not make themselves.

—Note taped to the office fridge

THE JAM

Despair is another way
of saying the copier has jammed
again and there is no one

who knows enough to fix it
but me. Copy after copy,
it is light that defines.

Do not ask me how it works—
magnets and tiny gears—
but again the same place sticks.

At least that small consistency.

Having counted the latches
and levers, moved them one by one,
I ask myself: *How many times*
must this be done?

Just the other day I heard
of a woman crushed to death
by her office door.

Killed by a faulty hinge. An oversight.
Little pieces run or ruin the world.

Somewhere an office worker
on a hillside seeks a higher purpose.
Somewhere the last business card
is being handed over.

Everything breaks.

The cover must be removed,
the insides taken out,

and into the dark
with the only fingers God has given me,
I still must reach.

SMALL TALK

Nature abhors a long silence.
—Lewis Thomas, *The Lives of a Cell*

Bird calls are mostly business: *Starling here.*
This is my tree!
Mind the cat in the underbrush.
Who does not love me and want to mate with me?

I would not think there could be time
for song, what with seasons to comprehend,
warnings to give, and the wide blue space
to navigate. Between idle chit chat

music rises—termites pound the earth,
hundreds of mammalian feet drum,
beetle wings tick against glass,
the proboscis of the moth emits its reedy sound.

I read that leeches have been heard
to tap rhythmically on leaves.
Earthworms, too, are not mute, intoning
their one note in the dirt.

Birds have their share of announcement
and agenda. But then comes pleasure—
the run and trill, the redundancy of joy
for which I am never quite prepared.

Flight and freedom, my little lice-ridden symbols,
clinging to the barely there branch,
shitting as you please. How you call out
when one alone has escaped death again.
How dangerously sweet you sing.

THE ARK

Building it was the easy part.
Noah just did what he was told:
so many cubits, a window here, more gopher wood.

But it was what he had to do next,
before the smiting began, poor schmuck,
with a goat under each arm,

herding cats, tortoises, and every
slow-moving creature
toward the very near end of everything . . .

Handpicking two worms from a tangle of bodies,
he must have wondered
what any of this had to do with saving civilization,

watching his sons wrestle alligators,
or his wife nudge a pair of ducks
up the plank with her dirty sandal.

All the chosen on board, the door sealed shut,
all his sons and their annoying wives
bickering over who should clean the elephant cage next.

Seasickness. Stench. His wife chiding him
about how to steer the god-forsaken boat.
And then the part the Boss had glossed over,

the "other duties as assigned," which meant waiting,
not yet having a good story to tell,
no rainbows whatsoever, no stupid doves,

waiting in the dark with its animal heat,
the work of rebuilding not yet begun,
not even yet imagined—waiting

with the others he loathed
and loved quietly, their stink and dread adrift
on the surface of the blue, fathomless world.

THE PENCIL

I have known the inexorable sadness of pencils.
—Theodore Roethke, "Dolor"

Pressed imper-
manently into
its diminishment,
ground down,
a tidy tool,
to dullness,
it is chewed
& chewed,
a spongy pulp,
leaden vein,
schoolchildren's
neat nubbin,
companion of
accountants,
riding high
in chest pocket,
perched above
an ear, stabbed into
the heart
of a woman's thick
coil of hair,
an awl of all
that stitches with gray
discursive thread
our lives—
with it the child
traces & erases
one stiff hesitant
letter then the next

THE COST

Each year the sun burns closer to the skin
and the skin yields to it.

Beneath the sink poison waits
with its childproof cap.

The dog sharpens his teeth
on the bone you gave him.

Herein lies a household of disasters
no insurance can save you from.

It takes a little more to get ahead, put the kids
in shoes, drive them toward the schoolyard

and leave them there. Those lessons
are harder than you remember.

No greater chance of death than at home,
or near it, but nothing is more dear.

Home Sweat Home hangs the unfortunately true
needlepoint above the door you pass through.

At dinner the dog panhandles
for table scraps and the children comply,

taking the meat off your plate and flinging it
to the floor. Each year more costly,

the bread, the milk. In the driveway
the sweet stench of antifreeze pooling.

The eyes strain to read the same story.
The top shelf is always higher than you can reach.

Each night the old tom fights less and less,
purring on your pillow with such violence

you can't hear anything else. There is a cost
to living, a frayed cuff, a deficit.

The receipts are totaled, then quickly lost.
Whatever you must pay, you pay.

BIG CHIEF NO LONGER WANTS TO BE BOSS

Chief wants a cubicle with a wilted prayer plant where he can hear Gladys mutter all day, pacing back and forth in her stocking feet. He wants to lunch in the break room and complain loudly about the person who brought trout. He wants a name badge with a bad photo and an extension where he can be reached at all times. He wants to battle the copy machine and open his own mail. He wants to drink using those small cups from the cooler and smack his lips in satisfaction. He wants a job description with other duties as assigned. He wants to steal a pen or two, a ream of paper, which he considers his due. He wants a commute that takes him directly home. He wants to grouse about the boss who is never there.

BIG CHIEF TAKES A VACATION

Chief is cruising to the Bahamas. Chief is taking a train to the Grand Canyon. Chief is biking the wine country. Chief is visiting his mother in Omaha. Chief is working on a novel. Chief is volunteering with the shelter. Chief is taking a cooking class. Chief is driving to Canada. Chief is touring the museums. Chief is at a conference on the East Coast. Chief is checking himself into rehab. Chief is learning to become a midwife. Chief is snorkeling in Hawaii. Chief is meditating in New Mexico. Chief is studying Italian. Chief is breaking the world record for pogo-sticking. Chief is adopting a baby girl from China. Chief is fighting fires in Montana. Chief is getting in touch with his roots. Chief is showing schoolchildren how to say *no* to drugs. Chief is starring in a reality television show. Chief is interviewing for the director position at a prison in Juneau, Alaska. Chief is getting a chemical face peel and will return to work in a few days a whole new man.

BIG CHIEF CONSIDERS THE EXACT LOCATION OF HIS HEART

Who has time to care about people's feelings? Chief wants to know. This is a workplace, not your grandmother's house. No one asks him if he feels like going to meetings. No one asks him if he really wants to pay his bills. If you want to have feelings, have them on your own time. That's your business, not mine, thinks Chief. There is a budget to balance and schedules to keep. A heart is a tool for pumping blood, for keeping the body warm, and it is a mistake to call it the seat of love. Who thought of that crap, Chief wants to know. *Gladys*, Chief calls out, *figure out who came up with that crap. About hearts and love.*

INTERVIEW FOR POSITION OF MYTHOLOGICAL HERO

First, tell the committee what interested you
in this job. Was it the Golden Fleece benefits,
the flexible hours, the opportunity for travel?

This is an entry-level position, but our company
is known for taking care of its people
and promoting from within. We're all family here.

There are so many things you could do with your time:
be a serf, perhaps, or a shepherd in the fields.
With us, though, there is a chance for greatness.

This is not just a paycheck. You must think of this
as an investment. Give us your life,
and we will return, in kind, immortal glory.

There are many requirements, of course.
Do you have any experience with labyrinths?
How did you get along with your previous coworkers?

If you were faced with the Minotaur,
what would you do first? Please describe in detail
your relationship with your mother.

Where do you see yourself an eternity from now?
How do you feel about tragedy?
Would you consider yourself a perfectionist?

Are you willing to take an arrow to the heart?
Are you willing to relocate?
Tell us one thing you did last year to rid the world of evil.
Tell us your plan, if you will, for pleasing the gods.

ATTN: TO WHOEVER LEFT FISH UNCOVERED IN THE OFFICE FRIDGE FOR THREE WEEKS, THINK OF OTHERS!!

There are many ways to start a war.
Take, for example, his assistant's short-short skirts.

Or the sign on the bathroom door that reads,
If you sprinkle when you tinkle
Be a sweetie, wipe the seat-ie!

No wonder no one likes poets.

Meanwhile, paper clips disappear
into a parallel universe,
your stapler each morning is turned
ever so slightly to the left—it's psychological warfare!

Soon enough all whispers sound like your name.
You are blamed for the broken coffee pot, and as a result
it will be months before the others look you in the eye.

How hard is it to replace the toilet paper roll?
Isn't that what we mean by *community?*

Above the cubicles, little flags of dominion,
little flags of surrender, but no one will tell you
which is which. The intern says something
about "economies of scale." Because of this
we avoid him in the lunchroom.
(He won't last long.)

Here the accountant's perfume creates
a hostile work environment. Someone is going
to HR about the dead plant in the corner.

Some rules should never need to be explained.
In the afternoon, the microwave chimes, and someone
distributes handfuls of popcorn, a bag
of fluffy and butter-soaked aneurysms we all can share.

THE ANIMAL KINGDOM REJECTS HUMAN COMPARISONS

If only you were truly a weasel,
slender predator, earning by tooth
and nail your victory dance.

Or like the chicken, capable of living
headless for hours (days sometimes)
scratching around without fear.

Cockroaches, particular in their habits,
have worn the same stylish exoskeleton
for millennia. It's human touch

they find revolting. To be called a pig
should be flattery. Only occasionally
and in captivity do they eat their young.

If you were a rat, you'd never call in sick,
having spread the plague and survived.
The snake in the grass wants nothing

to do with your shortcomings.
Of all the leeches, few suck blood.
And who are we to blame them

for holding on to a good thing?
Nature, yes, is cruel
but orderly. It gets the job done.

A bitch is just a female dog.
The ass at least cannot reproduce itself.
A fly feasts on shit and is unspeakably glad.

[OUT OF OFFICE REPLY]

I knew you would miss me
once I was gone.

❋

The keys you are looking for
are in the bottom drawer
on the right beneath the Kleenex.
Tell G. I will love her always.

❋

As suspected:
The world conspires to carry on
without me.

OLD BOSSES IN HEAVEN

They still don't know how it happened,
how all of you left them, not just the employees
with their "personal situations,"
but also the right-hand men of youth,
their apple shine and unbearably good jokes.
And who thought that Girl Friday of breath,
rushing in and out of the room
bearing news and notes from the latest meeting,
would have gone so soon?
Someone should have informed them
of the eventualities of death.
A memo, at least. *Hello?*
Heaven, it appears, is the vacation
they never took, and here they are,
supervisors all, stuck forever
in Bermuda shorts, wishing for sunglasses
throughout eternity.
In the field they have set up a boardroom
to confer over this serious matter—
assessment and strategy, a cost analysis of the hereafter.
But all they can remember is the others leaving—
a box turtle limping away from the backyard pond,
the cockatiel spouting, "Sorry, Charlie,"
from the telephone wire, all the pets of their childhoods,
the collie that ran away at every chance
until finally it was hit by a van and still
dragged itself another block from home before dying.
They can't understand how every living thing
found the open door irresistible,
even the body that turned in its letter
with an easy, unfaithful flick of the wrist.

STASIMON

Your mother doesn't work here.

—Note taped above office sink

EMPLOYEES MUST WASH HANDS

Employees must wash hands.
They must loosen their waistbands.

They must punch some extra hours.
They must throw more bridal showers.

They must fill up the gas tank.
They must file and they must rank.

They must brew the coffee strong.
They must sort out right from wrong.

They must jilt their lovely brides.
They must carefully pick sides.

They must speak in tongues of fire.
They must change the flattened tire.

They must push the rock uphill.
They must train the intern Phil.

They must bend or they will break.
They must order chocolate cake.

They must weep for what was lost.
They must purchase dental floss.

They must practice their headstands.
Employees must wash hands.

They must diagnose his gout.
They must serve up sauerkraut.

They must catch him in the act.
They must criticize with tact.

They must do as they are told.
They must build their own stronghold.

They must pay the meter maid.
They must brag of getting laid.

They must couch the threat in jest.
They must educate the rest.

They must muscle up the will.
They must take the load downhill.

They must give up a career.
They must trudge by year to year.

They must write a symphony.
They must breast-feed the baby.

Employees must wash hands.
They must start a garage band.

They must ask him for a raise.
They must laugh at his clichés.

They must lose the baby weight.
They must work a little late.

They must attend Suzie's wake.
They must watch their salt intake.

They must fix the jammed machine.
They must slurp up more caffeine.

They must never show their fear.
They must flaunt their bright headgear.

They must push the rock uphill.
They must fight about his will.

They must juggle flaming swords.
They must piss off their landlords.

They must solo in the choir.
They must threaten to retire.

They must crush the old beer cans.
Employees must wash hands.

They must clean the outdoor pool.
They must think that she's a fool.

They must put the past aside.
They must get their gray hair dyed.

They must merit praise and dread.
They must feign to be well read.

They must fix the toilet clog.
They must train the stupid dog.

They must weekend at the lake.
They must take a coffee break.

They must keep from standing still.
They must let it roll downhill.

They must buy a bigger boat.
They must edit the footnote.

They must ridicule the snob.
They must take another job.

Employees must wash hands.
They must dream of distant lands.

They must wish for many things.
They must choose the right earrings.

They must sweep the Persian rug.
They must change the bad sparkplug.

They must pluck the sliver out.
They must hold the sauerkraut.

They must contain multitudes.
They must cater to her moods.

They must moan but not distract.
They must land the new contract.

They must take another spill.
They must push it back uphill.

They must hand off the report.
They must offer up support.

They must cope as best they can.
They must take it like a man.

They must gently make demands.
Employees must wash hands.

They must operate this week.
They must test the new technique.

They must fire and they must freeze.
They must dream of calories.

They must take the righteous path.
They must give the dog a bath.

They must disregard the lies.
They must straighten their neckties.

They must ask for the day off.
They must fake a nasty cough.

They must take another pill.
They must push the rock uphill.

They must curl up into sleep.
They must toil and they must reap.

They must send the kids away.
They must wait for next payday.

EXODE

For when his day's work is done his business more properly begins.

—Christopher Smart, "Jubilate Agno"

ELEGY FOR A BRIEFCASE

The little latches cluck
with symmetry.
Get to work. Get to work.
How the combination lock keeps
its tiny secrets closed.

What poor cow gave up its hide
for you? Not a shoe
that goes places but a case
that must be filled.

Maybe inside there is a spare tie,
a sigh, a family portrait
cut down to business-card size.

Two leathered lips sealed shut
sit beside the door each day
like a dog ready to bolt.

How you have been heaved-ho,
how my father swung you
through the revolving door
until he went gray,
until part of his body
was cut away.

O brief briefcase, who was the man
that carried you?
His grip on you—tell me—
how much did he fear?

ON TRAGEDY

After ten thousand years of domestication, the goat,
bred for milk and meat, will have gnawed small trees
down to nubs, feeding on whatever comes its way.

In life, it will blunder down the grassy path,
and in death the tough hide will carry wine
or be turned to parchment for someone else to pen a song.

Lazing away in petting zoos, mauled by grubby hands,
no wonder they now graze and faint for fun,
nibble at the straw-colored braid of a child.

On hillsides the dark, insatiable gullets are herded.
Like the man who, piecemeal over seven years, ate a car,
they will take what you give them and transform it.

KINGDOM. PHYLUM. CLASS. ORDER. FAMILY. GENUS. SPECIES.

After cataclysm, there is work to be done,
dragging our poor selves out of the muck
single file into species, genus, family, etc.

Do you think this happened by accident?
Self-awareness, language, fire?
No. Someone had to taste the plant
to see if it was poisonous first.
Someone had to discover
cause and effect the hard way.

Climbing the hominid ladder, using tools and adverbs,
we've acquired certain marketable skills.
But let's not let it go to our proportionately sized heads.

Even cells are orderly,
little industrial neighborhoods
of cytoplasm and ribosomes,
each lugging its own operations manual
through the ages.

In a drop of pond scum, there is so much opportunity
for growth, a workforce of bacteria commuting
across the infinite void of the microscope's slide.

Such teamwork—cellular, subatomic—they all matter.
No "but I'm just a single cell" excuse.

Let's thank our lucky chromosomes
for binomial nomenclature,
for the mighty mitochondria
and the vacuoles who take out the trash,

all those unseen laborers
who put the *organism*
in *organization*.

These are the flagella whipping us into shape
and the long haul of biological persistence.

One hundred trillion micromanagers push us, slowly,
up the chain of being.

Determination. Responsibility. Love.
A highly developed brain capable of deception.

Drifting through the galaxy, we carry our empty spaces
through the empty spaces. A kingdom
of chemical reactions and impulses.
A government of dust.

COWORKERS

A tree is lovely, but the forest is dark and fire prone.

One cockroach is a nuisance. Three is a plague.

*

Too many beautiful days like this one,
and we'll have ourselves a drought.

Gone too long, and the ground resists what rains do come.

*

It's God's fault. I've been set up to fail.

How easily bacteria multiply.

*

One cough is a clearing.

How we pass around the flu.

*

It is a rule. The clocks are never set to the same time.

Upstream, salmon burst at the seams. They have given their all for the team.

AFTER THE BREAKDOWN IN COMMUNICATION, THERE IS THE REQUIRED SENSITIVITY TRAINING

The cat snaps the neck first
before it devours its prey.

Don’t take this the wrong way.

ON BEING LET GO

It's an orderly process: any part unable to survive the cold must be shed. Shorter days, longer nights signal that a tree must prepare itself, take what nutrients it can, drain leaves of chlorophyll and seal off veins that carry sap. The separation layer forms as cells soften at the base, a wound but also a means of protection. Color comes from this and from what is already there, masked behind green during the growing season. Through abscission and loss, the leaves become fire, crimson, gold. One by one, they are let go, a chemical shift in perspective. These are the deciduous trees growing in temperate climates where summers are warm and winters cool. The word comes from the Latin *decidere:* to choose, to cut off, cut down, cut out. If only we could decide, too, where we fall.

TO SERVE IS THE HIGHEST FORM OF LOVE

When the copier jams, love.
When your boss of six years misspells your name in a memo, love.
When someone absconds with the Pop-Tart from your desk that you've been saving for a day just like today, love.
Love, when, over the cubicles and the sound of phones ringing, you can hear Carl burping again and again.
When you can't say anything because you need the paycheck, love.
When you're sent home because you wore the red polo instead of the purple polo.
When the accountant tells you to speak up, have more confidence, show some fire in the belly, love.
When you've hidden your loathing for certain coworkers so well that you forget which ones you truly despise.
When you are scolded publicly for not cleaning out the fridge.
When, because of your way with words, you become the person to write all condolences on behalf of the office.
When, because you get along with everyone, you're moved into the cubicle next to Carl.
Love, when a note taped to your computer monitor says, "You forgot to water the plants."
Or when the woman who had you pick up her dry cleaning tells you of her miscarriage.
When the elevator stops working and you must run up and down three flights of stairs delivering the boss's mail.
When the new hire is the same as the old fire.
When you can no longer use "I statements," so you keep your mouth shut.
When the plaque promoting "excellence" needs to be dusted and you are the only one who notices.
When you are finally promoted and supervise three others and not one of them likes you, love.
When you toss out the perfume the others think smells like cat urine, love.
Love, when you keep a black sweater in your bottom drawer because the others prefer the thermostat to polar freeze.
Love, when that same sweater comes in handy for the occasional funeral.

When you are not invited to the bridal shower but must address the invites.
When you turn the radio down without resentment the first time someone asks.
When you stay late, love.
When you don't leave because you fear it could only get worse, love.
Love, when you think you can do better than this.
When no one notices you've been sick, love.
When everyone notices you haven't been returning voice mail, love.
When you quit but come back to work part-time as needed because at least you know
  now what needs to be done.
Love, even when you think you know how it ends.

THE BABIES ARE COMING

The babies are coming.
They are almost here.
They are here for our jobs and blood,
they'll lasso us with umbilical cords
and turn us blue.

O mothers and fathers of the world,
they are here to replace us,
slinking and slurping in dirty nappies,
gumming the doorknobs of office buildings,

and they will not be satisfied,
not with a breast or a song,
not with truckloads of toys,
not until they have slobbered the whole town and its citizens,
until they have smashed all industry,
like a block castle, to smithereens.

The babies will have us,
in suits and skirts, hamstrung with love.
We will give them names,
and they in turn, just learning to speak,
will point their chubby fingers
at the door and spout the first word,
which will be *surrender*.

They will take everything,
having survived the worst,
forced from their dark world
into this one we've created.
Asleep on the laps of executives,
they will rule the world
from the highest floors.

Squinting into daylight,
our mess of streets
and parking tickets,
the dented trash bins: for this
they will make us pay,
the world that sounds nothing
like the low drumming of blood
we promised them.

HOPELESSLY RUBBING TWO PIGS TOGETHER

It's not an easy maneuver.
To find two pigs
and rub them together.
I said *maneuver*.

You must not lose hope.
If you are confident,
it can be done.

Select the perfect swine
and get to work.

Inspiration comes
to those who seize the pig
and the other pig.

Many have tried
and failed. Give everything
you have to the pigs
and to the hopeless endeavor

of rubbing them together.
Nothing is hopeless.

THE TAKE-THIS-JOB-AND-SHOVE-IT ODE

Soon the children will come home having learned
new obscenities to hurl at each other
across the cul-de-sac, meaning "end of the road,
bottom of the sack that is your body."
Division and subdivision, each weekend
there is a new fence hewn from raw wood
that draws more hornets, too many wind chimes
at the mercy of weather. Your son has a puzzle
in a frame with one piece missing
that he pushes around and around
trying to make a picture. Your dog lacks control
and greets you so ferociously you fear
one day he will turn on you and eat your face.
What other life did you think was possible?
Sit down, you're having spaghetti again, and yes,
you must finish it. There are days when you are the best human
humanly possible. And then there are all the others.
Failure, you will say in your next interview,
is an opportunity. Like the open window a bird flew in
was an opportunity for the lazy house cat.
You want to scream, *Because of you I'm ruined!*
You have not slept well this past decade.
At the office, there is a cake that spells out *FAREWELL*.
It is loaded with frosted roses
and it would be a shame not to partake.
A coworker confides: *It's only the first and last*
weeks that they even take note of you.
They, meaning management, handing you a balloon
and an engraved pen, smiling.
You are closer to the last week of your life
than the first, so squalling naked in a crowded room
would be hardly appropriate now.

Your boss once said, *Don't you ever think?*
And you thought, I will have my revenge,
not like the others. I will take retirement
from these sons and daughters of bitches and never
look back. There is no sense explaining
to a beetle what it means to be you,
to get your kind of mail, to feel the electricity
upsurging through your joints every time you rise from bed.
The sun goes down and everyone heads into
separate living rooms to watch different shows.
With such flickering, you might think
we have something in common. Oh, we do.
The boss is the same everywhere and for everyone,
an asshole in a black suit holding a flaming cake,
coming closer and closer, and beyond that, the door.

LAST PRAYER

The drive is not accessible, Lord.
Format me, O God.

Should I save the changes I've made?
Do I really want to quit?

Forgive me, for I have performed
an illegal operation. Again.

I'm frozen, Lord. I cannot go back.
Copy and paste me to your will.

Save this draft. Save this draft.
Save this—

AUBADE FOR THE NEXT WEEK

All night long we push the rock uphill.
We are not the stuff of mythology.

Skin and bones, we flake into bed sheets,
filing dream paperwork into metal drawers,

rehearsing the ceremony of our worth.
The day's corridor is full of nameplates and doorways,

institutions that act as though they could survive
without us. We pick and choose

what we are willing to sell and dress ourselves.
Meanwhile phones ring, keys are turned

in their locks. We fall in love with hands
that brush away the minutes like flies.

How can we do better? We rise
and shake the clothes from their piles.

Traveling uphill both ways through time,
we never truly arrive or know it.

We are heroes to no one. What terrifying dreams
we have will most likely never happen.

Tragedy? Perhaps that too.
New light forces again through blinds:

we will not go on forever,
though mornings like this it feels we must.

ACKNOWLEDGMENTS

I owe a debt of gratitude to Carla, who inspired this collection when she snuck into my cubicle, lowered her voice, and said conspiratorially, "You should write about *this*."

Thank you to the following journals in which these poems were originally published, sometimes in slightly different versions:

"Attn: To Whoever Left Fish Uncovered in the Office Fridge for Three Weeks, THINK OF OTHERS!!" in *Seems*
"Employee Manual for Mortals" in *Willow Springs*
"Interview for Position of Mythological Hero" in *Mid-American Review*
"Old Bosses in Heaven" in *Burnside Review*
"On Metaphor" in *Grist*
"On Mythology" in *Poet Lore*
"Secretaries in Heaven" in *Juked*
"Small Talk" in *Hubbub*
"The Take-This-Job-and-Shove-It Ode" in *Baltimore Review*

The writing of this manuscript was funded in part by fellowships from the Arizona Commission on the Arts and the Oregon Arts Commission.

With thanks to those who have read and encouraged these poems along the way: Sally Ball, Bryan Fry, Emily Grosvenor, Heather Hummel, Charles Jensen, Robert Pinsky, Andrea Stolowitz, Dawn Diez Willis, and the Peregrine Writers: Eleanor Berry, the late Virginia Corrie-Cozart, Marilyn Johnston, Maggie Mayer, Ada Molinoff, Lois Rosen, Penina Taesali, Colette Tennant, Dina Triest.

My deepest gratitude belongs to my family who taught me what it means to work: Ian Johnson, Daryl Johnson, Linda Lenox, Walter Lenox, and Kathy Maurstad.

Thank you to Stephanie G'Schwind and the staff of The Center for Literary Publishing, and especially to Laura Kasischke, for choosing this book.

This book is set in Agency and Perpetua
by The Center for Literary Publishing
at Colorado State University.

Copyediting by Katie Naughton.
Proofreading by Melissa Hohl.
Book design and typesetting by KT Heins.
Cover design by Stephanie G'Schwind.
Cover art by Maria Luisa Corapi.
Printing by BookMobile.